The AI of War

Nathan McGrath

Also by Nathan McGrath

Nanopunk
Lightning Seed
Magic. A Rough Guide
Apocalypse Inc
Gingerbread dogs
The AI of War

Table of Contents

Introduction: The Unchanging Tao of Conflict in the Age of Sentient Code

The instruments of conflict may shift from bronze to algorithm, from sharpened spear to autonomous drone, yet the fundamental essence—the *Tao*—of warfare remains. It is, as it has ever been, a matter of grave consequence for the State; a domain of life and death, a path to either preservation or ruin, and thus a subject demanding the most meticulous study. While the advent of Artificial Intelligence (AI) heralds a profound transformation in the *character* of how wars are waged—altering speed, scale, and the very cognition of battle—it does not, in its current trajectory, upend the immutable *nature* of war itself. War remains a violent discourse, an interaction of opposing wills, fundamentally tethered to political objectives. To mistake a change in character for a change in nature is to court disaster, much like the Prussian generals who, clinging to the tactics of a bygone era, were undone by Napoleon's new way of war.

This treatise, therefore, seeks not to discard the ancient wisdom but to illuminate its enduring relevance in an age where calculations are performed by sentient code and decisions are augmented by machine intellect. The core tenet persists: victory flows from superior wisdom and strategy, not merely from possessing more formidable tools or greater computational might. The challenge lies in integrating the prodigious capacities of AI without succumbing to a purely technological view of conflict, for such a view risks obscuring the human, political, and ethical dimensions that continue to define it.

AI offers the allure of lifting the "fog of war" through unprecedented data processing and predictive power. Yet, this very complexity can birth new uncertainties. The opacity of certain algorithms, the potential for inherent biases, the vulnerability to sophisticated cyber malfeasance, and the sheer volume of data AI can generate may paradoxically weave new threads into the tapestry of battlefield friction and fog. If AI systems are like black boxes, their internal logic is inscrutable even to their creators, and reliance upon them introduces a novel form of unpredictability. If their training data is skewed, their judgments will be flawed, leading to potentially catastrophic errors in targeting or assessment. If they can be deceived or their data streams corrupted, they become conduits for enemy manipulation. And if they provide more information than a human commander can meaningfully process, decision paralysis, not clarity, may result. Thus, the promise of AI must be tempered with a profound understanding of its potential to create new forms of friction, demanding novel approaches to command and control. The art of war in the age of AI is the art of harnessing intelligent machines while mastering these new complexities, ensuring that technology serves strategy, and strategy serves the enduring political aims of the State.

I. Laying Algorithmic Plans: The Five Constants Recalibrated

Before the first drone is launched or the first line of malicious code deployed, the wise commander engages in deep calculation, assessing the fundamental factors that govern the outcome of conflict. These five constants, timeless in their essence, demand recalibration for an era dominated by artificial intelligence.

1. **The Moral Alignment (*Tao*):** Traditionally, this signifies the harmony between the ruler and the people, ensuring their willingness to follow him into danger. In the age of AI, this concept expands significantly. It now encompasses the ethical architecture of autonomous systems, their alignment with human values, international humanitarian law (IHL), and the rules of engagement. Public and allied trust in the probity and legality of AI-driven warfare is paramount. An AI that acts, or is perceived to act, unethically or unlawfully can shatter domestic consensus, fracture alliances, and hand potent propaganda victories to the adversary. The "Moral Alignment" thus demands rigorous ethical programming, transparent operational protocols, and a clear delineation of human responsibility to ensure AI actions consistently serve the state's legitimate political objectives and moral standing. Failure in this domain is

not merely a technical or legal lapse; it is a strategic vulnerability of the highest order. If a state's AI is seen as indiscriminately lethal or inherently biased, the accord with its populace and its international partners will fray, undermining any alliance, national support, or even the very will to fight, regardless of the AI's technical sophistication.

2. **The Digital Heaven** (*Tian*)**:** Sun Tzu spoke of Heaven as the interplay of night and day, cold and heat, times and seasons. In the AI era, "Heaven" can be considered as the dynamic, often volatile, environment of the digital and electromagnetic domains. It includes network latency, available bandwidth, computational cycles, and the relentless march of software updates and hardware obsolescence. The "weather" of this domain comprises the ever-shifting landscape of cyber threats, denial-of-service attacks, and electronic warfare. The "seasons" are the cycles of technological advantage, where a breakthrough by one side can temporarily grant dominance, only to be countered by the adversary's innovation. Understanding the opportune moment to act—when networks are optimal, when the adversary's systems are vulnerable, or when a new algorithm offers a fleeting edge—is crucial.
3. **Networked Earth** (*Di*)**:** The classical understanding of Earth involved distances, terrain, and defensible positions. The "Networked Earth" of AI warfare is the vast, interconnected cyber-physical landscape. This terrain includes physical data centres, undersea fibre

optic cables, satellite constellations, cellular networks, the logical architecture of the internet, cloud infrastructures, and the data streams upon which AI thrives. Chokepoints are no longer just mountain passes but critical network hubs or vulnerable software dependencies. Secure pathways are encrypted communication channels and hardened servers. The "ground" can be the data: vast datasets for training AI, or critical intelligence databases. To master this terrain is to understand its vulnerabilities, points of control, and the pathways to project digital power or interdict the enemy's.

4. **The Human-AI Commander** (*Jiang*): The commander's virtues of wisdom, sincerity, benevolence, courage, and strictness remain essential. However, leadership in the AI era requires new dimensions of expertise. The Human-AI Commander must possess a deep understanding of AI's capabilities and, critically, its limitations. They must cultivate trust within human-AI teams, manage the cognitive load AI can impose, and retain meaningful human control over the application of force, especially lethal force. This involves not just issuing commands, but understanding the AI's reasoning (where possible), recognising potential biases in its outputs, and making the ultimate moral and tactical judgments. Assessing the adversary's AI leadership—their skill in integrating AI, the quality of their human-AI teaming, and their doctrinal sophistication—becomes as important as evaluating their troop numbers or weaponry.

5. **Method and Protocols** (*Fa*): This encompasses the organisation, doctrine, training, and logistics that underpin military strength. In AI warfare, "Method and Protocols" translate to the entire AI Ecosystem. This includes robust software development pipelines, rigorous data governance and security, advanced cybersecurity protocols, effective AI training methodologies (including red-teaming and bias mitigation), and the logistical chains that support these complex systems (e.g., power, cooling, specialised personnel). Neglecting any aspect of this AI Ecosystem—from the quality of training data to the ethical guidelines governing AI deployment—creates foundational weaknesses that an astute adversary will exploit. A state might possess advanced algorithms, but these tools will be brittle and ineffective without the supporting infrastructure, skilled workforce, and sound doctrine.

The intricate dance of these five factors in the AI era highlights a new level of interconnectedness. A cyber-attack (an event in the "Networked Earth") can cripple cloud processing capabilities (a feature of the "Digital Heaven"), thereby neutralising sophisticated AI tools dependent on them. Planning must therefore account for such cascading effects. Similarly, a failure in "Moral Alignment," such as an AI causing significant unintended civilian harm, can have repercussions across all other factors, eroding public support, straining alliances (affecting "Method and Protocols" through reduced data sharing or interoperability), and providing the enemy with information warfare advantages. Strategic success hinges on a holistic mastery of these recalibrated constants.

II. Waging War with Data and Code: The Economy of Algorithmic Conflict

Sun Tzu taught that prolonged warfare drains the state, benefiting no nation. This wisdom finds new resonance in the age of algorithmic conflict, where the "costs" of war are redefined, and the demand for swift, decisive action is amplified by the very nature of the tools employed.

The sinews of AI warfare are not forged solely from steel and gunpowder, but from vast quantities of data, immense computational power, and the highly specialised human talent required to develop, deploy, and maintain these sophisticated systems. The expenditure in this new domain is relentless: servers consume enormous energy; algorithms require constant updates to remain effective against evolving countermeasures; hardware becomes obsolete at an astonishing pace; and the cognitive burden on human operators tasked with overseeing and interpreting AI outputs can be immense, leading to fatigue and error if not managed. These are the new logistics of war, where the "strategic rear" includes data centres, research laboratories, and university computer science departments.

The principle of efficiency, therefore, takes on heightened importance. Victory in AI-driven conflict may hinge on achieving decisive effects with the minimal expenditure of these precious digital resources—data, processing cycles, and human attention. Prolonged cyber engagements, where adversaries duel in the digital domain, can become wars of attrition, consuming computational resources and risking the exposure of valuable cyber tools and techniques. Similarly, autonomous systems locked in stalemates, requiring constant human intervention due to ambiguous environments or flawed programming, negate their intended speed and efficiency advantages.

The imperative for speed, a hallmark of sound military strategy, is further accentuated by AI. AI systems can observe, orient, decide, and act at speeds that dwarf human cognition. This acceleration compresses decision timelines dramatically. The commander who can leverage AI to process information faster, anticipate enemy actions more accurately, and deploy effects more rapidly gains a significant, potentially decisive advantage. However, this very speed introduces a perilous dynamic. The relentless pressure to accelerate decision cycles to match or exceed the pace of AI-driven operations can conflict directly with the need for careful deliberation, ethical consideration, and the maintenance of meaningful human control. "Flash wars," where automated systems engage and escalate at machine speed, potentially without complete human comprehension or intervention, become a tangible risk. An action taken by an AI in milliseconds, based on its interpretation of data, could trigger a cascading series of responses from an adversary's AI, leading to rapid, unintended escalation that outpaces diplomatic or even command-level intervention. The quest for speed, if not balanced by profound caution and robust control mechanisms, can thus lead to strategic instability.

The economy of AI warfare, therefore, is a delicate balance. It demands the efficient husbanding and allocation of digital resources, akin to managing traditional supply lines. It necessitates the pursuit of swift, decisive operations to avoid the drain of prolonged digital conflict. Yet, it also requires an acute awareness that the unbridled pursuit of machine-speed warfare can undermine strategic coherence and escalate conflicts beyond rational control. The wise commander in the age of AI understands that true economy lies not just in the efficient use of algorithms, but in the judicious application of force, guided by clear political objectives and an unwavering commitment to human oversight.

III. Attack by Algorithm and Deception: Subduing the Enemy's Mind and Machines

As Sun Tzu teaches, the acme of skill is to subdue the enemy without fighting. In an era where societies and militaries are deeply interwoven with digital systems and reliant on the flow of information, this highest form of victory finds potent new expression through attacks targeting the adversary's cognitive and digital foundations. AI provides the means to wage such campaigns with unprecedented sophistication and scale.

"All warfare is based on deception," a maxim that gains new dimensions in the digital age. The commander skilled in AI warfare will feign computational weakness while masking true algorithmic strength, or simulate network vulnerabilities to lure an adversary into digital ambushes. AI can generate misleading activity patterns, spoof sensor data, or create "ghost" forces in the digital domain, diverting enemy attention and resources. The modern battlefield extends into the cognitive realm, where AI-driven information operations seek to manipulate perception, sow discord, and erode the enemy's will to resist.

This attack on the enemy's mind and machines can take several forms:

1. **AI-Driven Cyber Warfare:** Algorithms can identify

vulnerabilities in enemy networks with superhuman speed, deploy tailored malware, disrupt critical infrastructure, and corrupt essential data. The aim is to degrade the enemy's ability to command, control, communicate, and compute, effectively blinding and paralysing them before kinetic force is even considered.

2. **Electronic warfare amplified by AI:** Intelligent systems can dynamically analyse the electromagnetic spectrum, identify enemy emissions, and deploy precise jamming or spoofing techniques to disable sensors, disrupt communications, and mislead navigation systems. This creates pockets of digital darkness or illusory realities for the adversary.
3. **Information and Psychological Operations at Scale:** AI excels at analysing vast datasets of public information to understand an adversary's societal fault lines, popular sentiments, and individual psychological profiles. This understanding allows for the crafting and disseminating of highly targeted disinformation and propaganda. The advent of "deepfakes", AI-generated synthetic media that can realistically impersonate leaders or fabricate events, presents an exceptionally potent tool for deception. A fabricated video of a commander issuing contradictory orders, or a political leader announcing a surrender that never happened, can sow chaos and undermine morale. While the laws of war distinguish between legitimate ruses and unlawful perfidy (e.g., feigning surrender to launch an attack), the speed and reach of AI-disseminated deepfakes challenge traditional enforcement and

verification.

4. **Attacking the Adversary's AI:** Perhaps the most sophisticated form of algorithmic attack is to target the enemy's AI systems directly. This can involve "data poisoning," where subtly corrupted data is fed into their training models, leading to flawed decision-making or biased outputs. It could mean exploiting vulnerabilities in their AI software, or manipulating sensor inputs to make their autonomous systems "see" a false reality. If an enemy's AI can be made to distrust its own perceptions or make consistently wrong predictions, its utility is nullified.

The true art of subduing the enemy without fighting in the AI era may lie in degrading their *trust* in their information and decision-making systems. If commanders become uncertain about the veracity of the data their AI provides, if soldiers doubt the reliability of their autonomous wingmen, or if the populace loses faith in the pronouncements of their leaders due to the pervasive threat of deepfakes, then the enemy's cohesion and operational effectiveness crumble from within. This cognitive paralysis, achieved through the subtle and persistent application of AI-driven deception and disruption, can be more devastating and strategically significant than the physical destruction of their forces. It is the modern equivalent of draining the water from the enemy's well, achieving victory by rendering their most advanced tools unusable through the erosion of belief in their integrity. This approach aligns with Sun Tzu's emphasis on attacking the enemy's strategy and alliances before resorting to attacking their armies or cities.

IV. Disposition of Intelligent Forces: Digital Invincibility and Vulnerability

Sun Tzu counsels that the skilled warrior first puts himself beyond the possibility of defeat, and then waits for an opportunity to defeat the enemy. In the age of AI, achieving this state of "digital invincibility" and recognising exploitable vulnerabilities in an adversary's digital posture are paramount. Strength is no longer measured solely by the number of autonomous platforms or the sophistication of algorithms, but by the resilience of one's AI foundation and the ability to discern and exploit weaknesses in the enemy.

Achieving Digital Invincibility:

Making oneself "invincible" in AI involves a multi-layered defence of the entire AI ecosystem. This begins with robust **cybersecurity** measures to protect networks, data centres, and individual AI systems from intrusion, manipulation, or denial of service. It requires **resilient network architectures** with redundancy and failover capabilities to ensure continuous operation even if parts of the infrastructure are compromised. **Secure and verified data storage** is crucial, with strong data provenance and integrity measures to prevent tampering or corruption, as AI systems are only as reliable as the data they are trained on and operate with.

Furthermore, the algorithms must be **well-tested, rigorously validated, and ethically aligned**. This includes processes to identify and mitigate inherent biases that could lead to flawed or discriminatory outcomes, thereby undermining trust and operational effectiveness. Where feasible, transparency and explainability contribute to this invincibility by allowing human operators to understand and trust AI decision-making and identify anomalies that might indicate compromise or malfunction. A proactive, dynamic defence posture is essential; static digital fortifications are insufficient against persistent and adaptive cyber threats. This involves active threat hunting, continuous monitoring, and rapid patching and updating of systems.

Perceiving and Exploiting Adversary Vulnerabilities:

Opportunity for the astute AI-enabled commander lies in the digital weaknesses of the adversary. These vulnerabilities can manifest in numerous ways:

- **Unpatched or outdated software and systems:** These provide entry points for cyberattacks.

- **Poorly trained or biased AI models:** These can be exploited if an adversary's AI exhibits predictable biases (e.g., in target recognition due to skewed training data). For instance, if an enemy's surveillance AI is known to under-identify targets with certain camouflage patterns, those patterns can be used to achieve surprise.

- **Reliance on insecure or easily disruptable networks:** Dependence on civilian communication infrastructure or unencrypted links creates vulnerabilities for electronic warfare or cyber-interdiction.

- **Data chokepoints:** Centralised data storage or processing nodes become high-value targets. Disrupting these can cripple the enemy's AI capabilities.

- **Lack of algorithmic diversity:** If an adversary relies heavily on a single type of AI model or algorithm, developing a countermeasure to that specific model can have a disproportionate impact.

- **Weak human-AI teaming practices:** If enemy operators do not trust their AI or their AI systems are poorly integrated into their decision-making processes, their overall effectiveness is reduced.

The line between offence and defence in AI warfare is often blurred. Defensive cybersecurity measures, such as active threat hunting, can involve actions within one's own networks that resemble offensive reconnaissance. Similarly, some offensive cyber operations may be undertaken pre-emptively to neutralise an imminent threat, thus serving a defensive purpose. The key is to secure one's own digital foundations so thoroughly that the enemy finds no easy purchase, while simultaneously developing the AI-driven intelligence and cyber capabilities to identify and exploit the inevitable cracks in the adversary's digital armour.

Data itself becomes a critical element of strategic disposition. Securing the quality, integrity, and access control of one's data is paramount for a robust defence, ensuring that friendly AI systems operate reliably. Conversely, gaining access to, understanding, and potentially manipulating the adversary's data through sophisticated AI-powered Intelligence, Surveillance, and Reconnaissance (ISR) or cyber means is key to identifying and creating offensive opportunities. Data poisoning, for example, where an adversary's AI training datasets are subtly corrupted, can be a strategic attack on their disposition, degrading their AI's capabilities from within, often without their immediate knowledge. In this new domain, controlling the informational high ground and ensuring the integrity of one's own digital terrain are as vital as controlling key geographical features in traditional warfare.

V. Algorithmic Force (Shi): The Momentum of Intelligent Systems

Sun Tzu speaks of *Shi*, often translated as strategic momentum, potential energy, or the disposition of force that creates an irresistible impetus, like logs and stones rolling down a steep mountain. In the age of AI, *Shi* is generated not just by mass and velocity in the physical domain, but by the accumulation of informational advantage, the speed and scale of algorithmic processing, and the capacity for AI-driven surprise.

The commander who understands algorithmic *Shi* seeks to build a preponderance of digital and cognitive advantages that, when unleashed, overwhelm the adversary's capacity to respond effectively. This involves several dimensions:

1. **Data Dominance:** Amassing superior quantities of relevant, high-quality, and diverse data for training AI models creates a foundational potential. An AI trained on a more comprehensive and accurate dataset will generally possess greater perception, prediction, and decision-making acuity. This data advantage, like a reservoir at high altitude, holds immense potential energy.
2. **Algorithmic Superiority:** Developing and deploying more advanced, efficient, and adaptive algorithms constitutes another form of *Shi*. An AI that can learn faster, adapt to novel situations more effectively, or

process information quicker and more accurately than the adversary possesses a critical edge. This superiority can allow for rapidly exploiting fleeting opportunities, creating a cascade of successes.

3. **Computational Capacity and Speed:** The ability to bring massive computational power to bear, enabling AI systems to operate at machine speed, generates momentum that can shatter an opponent's decision cycle. When one side can analyse, decide, and act orders of magnitude faster than the other, the slower side perpetually reacts, ceding the initiative and becoming vulnerable to surprise.
4. **Integration and Orchestration:** True algorithmic *Shi* arises not from individual AI systems operating in isolation, but from their seamless integration into a cohesive fighting force, orchestrated with human commanders and traditional assets. AI-enabled battle management systems that dynamically allocate resources, coordinate autonomous swarms, and synchronise multi-domain effects create a combined momentum far greater than the sum of its parts.
5. **The Element of Surprise through Novelty:** Deploying AI with novel capabilities or in unexpected ways can create a shock effect, disrupting the enemy's plans and psychological equilibrium. This could be an autonomous system exhibiting an unforeseen tactic, or an AI-driven cyber weapon with an unknown exploit. The surprise itself generates momentum, forcing the enemy onto the defensive.

The skilful commander cultivates this algorithmic *Shi* patiently, investing in the foundational elements of data, talent, and infrastructure. They understand that *Shi* is not merely about having AI, but about how that AI is positioned, trained, and prepared to act. When the moment is ripe, this accumulated potential is released, not as a blunt instrument, but as a precisely directed force, exploiting identified enemy weaknesses with overwhelming speed and intelligence. The aim is to create a situation where the adversary's AI and human decision-makers are so inundated, confused, or outpaced that their capacity for coherent action collapses. This is the essence of leveraging algorithmic force to achieve decisive outcomes.

VI. Weak Points and Strong in the Digital Domain (Xu Shi)

The principle of *Xu Shi*, identifying and striking the enemy's weaknesses (*xu* – empty, vulnerable) while protecting one's strengths (*shi* – complete, solid), is central to Sun Tzu's strategic thought. In the AI era, these points of emptiness and solidity are found in physical dispositions and, crucially, within warfare's digital and cognitive architectures.

Identifying Adversary Weaknesses (Xu):

The AI-enabled commander must be adept at discerning the vulnerabilities in an opponent's digital fabric. These "empty points" can include:

- **Software Vulnerabilities:** Unpatched operating systems, insecure applications, or flaws in bespoke military software create gateways for cyber intrusion and disruption. AI tools can rapidly scan for and identify such weaknesses across vast networks.

- **Algorithmic Bias and Predictability:** AI models trained on limited or biased datasets may exhibit predictable flaws in perception or decision-making. For instance, a target recognition AI that consistently misidentifies particular objects under specific conditions presents an exploitable weakness. Suppose an enemy's AI for predictive logistics consistently overestimates needs in one area and underestimates in another. In that case, this pattern can be used to mislead or strain their supply chain.

- **Data Dependencies and Chokepoints:** Over-reliance on a single data source, a centralised data processing hub, or specific communication links creates critical vulnerabilities. Disrupting these chokepoints can cripple an adversary's AI-dependent operations.

- **Insufficient or Compromised Training Data:** An AI's "knowledge" is derived from training data. If this data is incomplete, outdated, or subtly poisoned by an attacker, the AI's performance will be degraded, creating an "empty" capability.

- **Network Fragility:** Dependence on insecure civilian networks, lack of redundancy, or susceptibility to electronic warfare can isolate and render an adversary's AI systems ineffective.

- **Human Factor Vulnerabilities:** Weak cybersecurity practices among personnel, susceptibility to AI-driven social engineering, or a lack of trust between human operators and their AI systems can undermine even the most sophisticated technological defences.

- **Over-reliance on Automation:** An adversary who has become overly dependent on autonomous systems without sufficient human oversight or backup mechanisms may be vulnerable if those systems are disabled, deceived, or encounter novel situations they are not programmed to handle.

Consolidating One's Strengths (Shi):

Conversely, commanders must ensure their digital posture is "solid." This involves:

- **Resilient and Redundant Networks:** Architectures that can withstand attack and reroute data through multiple paths.

- **Well-Trained, Unbiased, and Robust AI:** Algorithms that have been rigorously tested, validated against diverse scenarios, and designed with bias mitigation techniques. This includes AI systems capable of functioning effectively in degraded or contested (e.g., GPS-denied) environments.

- **Diverse and Secure Data Sources:** Reducing reliance on single points of failure for data collection and ensuring the integrity and security of training and operational datasets.

- **Strong Human-AI Teaming:** Cultivating trust and effective collaboration between human personnel and AI systems, ensuring that AI augments human judgment rather than supplanting it unwisely. This includes clear protocols for human intervention and oversight.

- **Adaptive Cybersecurity:** Employing AI-driven cybersecurity tools that can detect and respond to novel threats in real-time.

- **Continuous Learning and Adaptation:** Implementing processes for AI systems and rules to learn from engagements and adapt to evolving threats and operational environments.

The art lies in concentrating one's "solid" AI capabilities against the enemy's identified "empty" points. This might mean launching a cyberattack against a known software vulnerability, using AI-generated deception to exploit a predictable bias in enemy sensor systems, or targeting a critical data link upon which their AI network depends. By understanding the interplay of *Xu* and *Shi* in the digital domain, the commander can avoid costly attrition and achieve decisive results through the precise application of AI-enabled force.

VII. Manoeuvring with Intelligent Agents (Jun Zheng)

Manoeuvre, the art of positioning forces to gain advantage before and during battle, takes on new dimensions with the advent of intelligent agents. AI enables the swifter and more precise movement of physical assets and novel forms of manoeuvre within the cyber and cognitive domains. The goal of manoeuvre, as Sun Tzu taught, is to make the difficult direct and to turn misfortune into advantage.

Physical Manoeuvre Enhanced by AI:

- **Autonomous Navigation and Obstacle Avoidance:** AI-powered unmanned systems (air, ground, and maritime) can navigate complex and hostile terrains, including GPS-denied environments, with greater autonomy and precision than ever before. This allows for infiltration into areas inaccessible to manned platforms, rapid reconnaissance, and the positioning of assets in advantageous locations without direct human piloting.

- **Swarm Coordination:** AI algorithms can coordinate the actions of large numbers of smaller, often expendable, autonomous systems (drone swarms). These swarms can manoeuvre collectively to overwhelm enemy defences, conduct distributed sensing, or execute complex, synchronised attacks from multiple axes, creating dilemmas for traditional defensive systems.

- **Optimised Logistics and Resupply:** AI can optimise routes and schedules for logistical support, ensuring that manoeuvring forces are supplied efficiently. Predictive analytics can anticipate needs, allowing for pre-emptive positioning of supplies and maintenance assets, thus sustaining the tempo of manoeuvre.

Cyber Manoeuvre:

The digital realm is a battlespace where AI agents can manoeuvre with stealth and speed:

- **Network Infiltration and Lateral Movement:** AI-driven cyber tools can autonomously probe enemy networks, identify vulnerabilities, and move laterally through compromised systems to reach high-value targets, such as command and control nodes or critical data repositories. This is akin to an army outflanking an enemy position to strike at its rear.

- **Dynamic Resource Allocation:** AI can manage the allocation of cyber weapons and network resources, shifting attack vectors or defensive postures in real-time based on the evolving situation and enemy responses.

- **Deceptive Manoeuvres in Cyberspace:** AI can create decoy network traffic, simulate the presence of forces where none exist, or lead enemy cyber defences on false trails, allowing genuine attack vectors to proceed unhindered.

Cognitive Manoeuvre:

AI also enables manoeuvre in the cognitive space, shaping the perceptions and decisions of the adversary:

- **Targeted Information Operations:** By analysing an adversary's information consumption patterns and psychological vulnerabilities, AI can help craft and deliver tailored messages designed to mislead, demoralise, or sow confusion. This is a manoeuvre to disrupt the enemy's decision-making cycle and undermine their cohesion.

- **Controlling the Narrative:** AI can rapidly generate and disseminate content across multiple platforms to shape the information environment, presenting a version of events favourable to one's side and countering enemy narratives. This is manoeuvring to seize the "informational high ground."

The challenge in manoeuvring with intelligent agents lies in achieving synchronisation across physical, cyber, and cognitive domains and maintaining coherence of effort towards the strategic objective. It also involves the risk of ceding too much initiative to autonomous systems, potentially leading to actions that are tactically successful but strategically misaligned. The skilled commander uses AI to enhance the speed, precision, and adaptability of manoeuvre, but always within a framework of clear intent and robust human oversight, ensuring that the "contention for advantage" ultimately serves the overall plan.

VIII. Variation in Algorithmic Tactics (Jiu Bian)

Sun Tzu emphasised the importance of tactical flexibility and adapting to circumstances, outlining "nine variations" or contingencies that a commander must master. In the era of AI, the capacity for tactical variation is exponentially increased, as algorithms can be designed to adapt, learn, and implement a vast array of responses based on real-time battlefield conditions. However, this also introduces new complexities in managing and predicting AI behaviour.

The "nine variations" can be reinterpreted for AI-driven warfare, not as fixed situations, but as categories of tactical adaptation and potential AI-related contingencies:

1. **On Dispersive Ground, Do Not Fight (with Uncoordinated AI):** If AI systems are isolated, unable to communicate or coordinate (e.g., due to jamming or network failure), avoid committing them to complex offensive actions where their individual efforts will be wasted. Focus on preserving them or using them for localised, independent tasks.
2. **On Facile Ground, Do Not Halt (Exploit Algorithmic Speed):** When AI provides a clear and rapid path to an objective (e.g., identifying a fleeting vulnerability), do not hesitate. Leverage the speed and decisiveness of AI-driven targeting or cyber

exploitation.

3. **On Contentious Ground, Do Not Attack (if AI is Disadvantaged):** If the adversary holds a superior AI position (e.g., better algorithms for the specific task, more robust cyber defences), avoid direct algorithmic confrontation. Seek to change the terms of engagement or find an alternative approach.
4. **On Open Ground, Do Not Block the Enemy's Way (but Monitor with AI):** Allow a retreating or reconfiguring enemy an avenue of escape, but use Intelligence, Surveillance, and Reconnaissance, AI-ISR to monitor their movements, gather intelligence on their new dispositions, and identify future vulnerabilities.
5. **On Ground of Intersecting Highways, Join Hands with Allies (and Ensure AI Interoperability):** In complex, multi-agent environments (e.g., coalition operations), ensure that friendly AI systems can communicate, share data, and deconflict actions. Lack of AI interoperability is a critical vulnerability.
6. **On Serious Ground, Plunder (Secure Data and Computational Resources):** When deep in contested digital territory or facing resource constraints, prioritise securing the data feeds, processing power, and network access necessary for your AI to function effectively. Deny these to the enemy.
7. **On Difficult Ground, Keep Steadily on the March (Maintain AI Resilience):** In challenging environments (e.g., heavy electronic warfare, high levels of cyberattack), ensure AI systems are resilient,

can operate in degraded modes, and have fallback mechanisms. Do not allow temporary setbacks to halt essential AI functions.

8. **On Hemmed-in Ground, Resort to Stratagem (Employ AI Deception):** If AI forces are constrained or at a tactical disadvantage, use AI-driven deception (e.g., spoofing, decoys, disinformation) to create openings or mislead the enemy about your intentions or capabilities.
9. **On Desperate Ground, Fight (Leverage AI for Last-Ditch Defence/Offence):** When facing critical threats with limited options, AI can be used for rapid, automated defensive responses (e.g., active protection systems) or to execute high-risk, high-payoff offensive actions where speed and precision are paramount.

Beyond these reinterpretations, AI introduces its own set of tactical variations and considerations:

- **Adaptive Algorithms:** Machine learning models can adjust their tactics based on ongoing analysis of enemy behaviour and success rates. This allows for a level of dynamic adaptation previously impossible.

- **Algorithmic Warfare Tactics:** This could include tactics like "algorithmic flanking" (using AI to find and exploit unconventional attack vectors in cyberspace), "data starvation" (denying an enemy AI the data it needs to function), or "bias exploitation" (designing tactics to trigger known biases in an adversary's AI).

- **Human-AI Tactical Teaming:** The way humans and AI collaborate on tactical tasks can vary greatly, from AI providing decision support to humans, to humans supervising autonomous AI actions, to fully autonomous AI operations in specific contexts. A key tactical variation is to choose the right teaming model for the situation.

- **Ethical Boundaries as Tactical Constraints:** The ethical programming of an AI will dictate the range of tactics it can employ. An AI constrained from specific actions for ethical reasons will have a different tactical playbook than one without such constraints.

The commander must understand the potential range of AI behaviours, both intended and emergent, and be prepared to intervene or adjust plans when AI-driven tactics are not achieving the desired outcomes or are creating unintended risks. The promise of AI is vast tactical flexibility, but its peril is complexity and the potential for actions that are locally optimal but strategically detrimental.

IX. The Army on the March (Digitally): Deployment and Movement of AI Assets (Xing Jun)

Sun Tzu's teachings on marching and encampment dealt with armies' physical movement and positioning to ensure their security and readiness. In the AI era, the "army on the march" also refers to deploying, updating, and sustaining digital assets and AI capabilities across a global, interconnected battlespace.

Deployment of AI Capabilities:

- **Software as Force Projection:** Deploying AI often means pushing software updates to existing hardware platforms (drones, vehicles, sensor systems) already in the field. A new algorithm that enhances target recognition or navigation can be "marched" to the front lines digitally, instantly upgrading the capabilities of numerous deployed assets. This allows for rapid adaptation and capability enhancement without physical reinforcement.

- **Edge Computing vs. Cloud Computing:** Decisions about where AI processing occurs (on the device at the "edge," or in centralised cloud data centres) are crucial deployment considerations. Edge processing reduces latency and reliance on communication links but may be limited by onboard computational power. Cloud processing offers greater power but introduces dependencies on network connectivity. The "march" may involve shifting processing loads based on the tactical situation and network availability.

- **Activation of Dormant Capabilities:** AI systems may be deployed with certain capabilities held in reserve, which are to be activated remotely when tactically advantageous or when specific threats emerge. This is a form of digital "ambush" or surprise.

Movement and Allocation of AI Resources:

- **Autonomous Platform Mobility:** The physical movement of AI-enabled unmanned systems (UAVs, UGVs, UUVs) remains a core aspect of their deployment. AI enhances their ability to navigate autonomously, avoid threats, and reach designated operational areas efficiently.

- **Dynamic Allocation of Computational Resources:** For AI systems reliant on cloud infrastructure, the "movement" of AI assets can mean reallocating server capacity, bandwidth, and processing power from one operational theatre or task to another based on shifting priorities. This requires a flexible and responsive digital infrastructure.

- **Securing Digital Supply Lines:** Just as traditional armies need secure supply lines for food and ammunition, AI-driven forces need secure and reliable data links, power sources, and access to updated software and threat intelligence. The "march" must account for the protection of these digital lifelines from enemy interdiction (cyberattacks, electronic warfare).

Encampment in the Digital Age (Establishing Secure AI Operational Environments):

- **Hardened Networks and Systems:** "Encamping" AI assets involves ensuring they operate from secure networks, with robust cybersecurity measures to prevent unauthorised access or manipulation.

- **Data Integrity and Availability:** Ensuring AI systems can access verified, uncorrupted data is critical for effective operation. This may involve establishing secure data repositories or redundant data feeds.

- **Monitoring and Maintenance:** Deployed AI systems require continuous monitoring for performance anomalies, potential compromises, or the need for updates. This is the digital equivalent of posting sentries and maintaining equipment.

- **Ethical and Legal Overwatch:** Even when "encamped" or operating autonomously within defined parameters, AI systems must remain under appropriate human oversight to ensure compliance with rules of engagement and ethical guidelines.

The "march" of AI assets is characterised by speed, flexibility, and new vulnerabilities. A critical software update intercepted and corrupted by an enemy, or a denial-of-service attack on a key data centre, can halt the digital advance as effectively as a physical obstacle could stop a traditional army. The commander must therefore plan the deployment and sustainment of AI capabilities with the same care and foresight applied to the movement of physical forces, always considering the security of the digital "terrain" and the resilience of the "supply lines" upon which these intelligent agents depend.

X. Terrain (Digital and Cognitive Landscapes) (Di Xing)

Sun Tzu meticulously categorised terrain, understanding how its characteristics could favour or hinder military operations. In the st century, the concept of terrain expands beyond the physical to encompass the intricate digital and cognitive landscapes where AI-driven conflict unfolds. Mastering these new terrains is as vital as understanding mountains and rivers were in ages past.

The Digital Terrain:

This is the "Networked Earth" previously introduced, but its features bear further examination as operational terrain:

- **Network Topology:** The architecture of global and local networks—including fibre optic cables, satellite links, cellular infrastructure, and internal military networks—forms the "ground" upon which digital forces operate. Understanding its pathways, chokepoints (e.g., major internet exchange points, critical servers), and redundancies is essential for planning cyber operations and ensuring resilient communications for AI systems.

- **Data Topography:** Vast datasets, whether structured or unstructured, form a kind of terrain that AI must navigate and exploit. This includes intelligence databases, sensor feeds, open-source information, and even the "data exhaust" of societies. Knowing where critical data resides, how it is protected, and how it flows is key to intelligence gathering and targeting.

- **The Electromagnetic Spectrum:** This is a contested terrain where wireless communication, sensor operations (radar, LiDAR), and electronic warfare occur. Dominance or denial of specific frequency bands can cripple an adversary's AI-dependent systems or protect one's own. AI itself can be used to dynamically manage spectrum usage and identify/counter enemy electronic attacks.

- **Cloud Infrastructure and Edge Devices:** The distribution of computational resources—from massive, centralised cloud data centres to small, embedded processors on edge devices (like drones or soldier-worn sensors)—defines another layer of terrain. Operations may require leveraging the power of the cloud or, in contested environments, relying on the localised capabilities of edge AI.

- **Software and Protocol Landscapes:** The specific operating systems, applications, and communication protocols used by an adversary constitute a terrain with vulnerabilities and characteristics. Exploiting flaws in this software terrain is a primary objective of cyber warfare.

The Cognitive Terrain:

Warfare also plays out in the minds of individuals and populations. AI provides powerful tools to understand and influence this cognitive terrain:

- **Information Environment:** The sum of information available to a population or a specific target group, including news media, social media, and interpersonal communications. AI can be used to analyse this environment, identify influential narratives and key communicators, and disseminate targeted messages.

- **Belief Systems and Psychological Profiles:** AI can assist in modelling the belief systems, cultural norms, and psychological vulnerabilities of adversary leaders, military units, or civilian populations. This understanding can inform psychological operations designed to erode morale, sow doubt, or encourage specific behaviours.

- **Human-Machine Interface as Terrain:** The way human operators interact with their AI systems (the displays, controls, and feedback mechanisms) is a form of cognitive terrain. Poorly designed interfaces can lead to information overload, misinterpretation, or slow response times, creating vulnerabilities that an enemy might exploit if they understand these limitations.

- **Trust and Reliance:** The level of trust that human operators place in their AI systems is critical to the cognitive terrain. If trust is too low, valuable AI capabilities may go unused. If trust is too high (automation bias), operators may fail to scrutinise AI recommendations adequately. Attacking this trust is a key objective of cognitive warfare.

Navigating these digital and cognitive terrains requires new forms of intelligence, reconnaissance, and manoeuvre. AI-powered tools are essential for mapping these complex landscapes, identifying advantageous "positions," and understanding the "lines of communication" that sustain friendly and enemy operations. Just as Sun Tzu advised adapting tactics to physical ground, the AI-era commander must adapt strategies to the unique characteristics of these intangible but critically important battlefields.

XI. The Nine Situations in AI-Driven Conflict (Jiu Di)

Sun Tzu described nine varieties of ground, or strategic situations, each demanding a specific response from the commander. These situations, born from the interplay of terrain, enemy disposition, and one's own condition, find parallels in the complex dynamics of AI-driven conflict. Adapting these classical situations to the modern context can provide a strategic and tactical decision-making framework when intelligent machines are integral to the fight.

1. **Dispersive Ground** (*San Di*)**:** *When AI assets operate within their own secure networks, but are not yet concentrated for a specific offensive operation.*

○ **AI Context:** AI systems perform routine surveillance, data collection, or defensive monitoring within well-protected digital enclaves. There is no immediate, unified offensive intent.

○ **Sun Tzu's Counsel (Adapted):** Do not fight to win, but focus on consolidating AI capabilities, ensuring data integrity, patching vulnerabilities, and maintaining a high state of algorithmic readiness. Avoid premature offensive actions that could reveal capabilities or invite counterattack before forces are digitally "arrayed."

1. **Facile Ground** (*Qing Di*): *When AI forces have made a shallow penetration into adversary networks or systems, with easy lines of retreat.*

○ **AI Context:** Initial cyber reconnaissance has yielded access, or autonomous scouts have gathered preliminary data from lightly defended enemy perimeters. Withdrawal is straightforward.

○ **Sun Tzu's Counsel (Adapted):** Do not halt. Exploit the opening rapidly with AI tools to gather further intelligence, map vulnerabilities, or conduct limited disruptive effects, but be prepared to disengage quickly if resistance stiffens. Avoid overextending AI assets into areas where support or exfiltration is uncertain.

1. **Contentious Ground** (*Zheng Di*): *Digital terrain or a specific AI capability that, if secured, offers a significant advantage to either side.*

○ **AI Context:** Control over a key communication node, a critical database, a superior AI algorithm for a specific task (e.g., electronic warfare), or the ability to neutralise a key enemy AI system.

○ **Sun Tzu's Counsel (Adapted):** Do not attack if the adversary's AI holds a clear advantage or if the cost of securing it is too high. If advantageous, use AI to seize and hold this "digital high ground" swiftly, employing surprise and overwhelming algorithmic force if necessary.

1. **Open Ground** (*Jiao Di*): *Network segments or data pathways where both sides have relatively free access and can observe each other's AI activities.*

○ **AI Context:** Public internet segments, shared coalition networks (with varying security levels), or areas where AI-driven ISR from both sides is prevalent.

○ **Sun Tzu's Counsel (Adapted):** Do not try to block the enemy's AI from observing (as this may be impossible or reveal your own methods), but ensure your own AI activities are either masked, deceptive, or designed to feed the enemy misleading information. Focus on robust AI-driven counterintelligence and operational security.

1. **Ground of Intersecting Highways** (*Qu Di*): *Critical junctures in digital infrastructure or AI ecosystems where alliances must be formed or interoperability is key.*

○ **AI Context:** Shared cloud platforms for multinational AI development, common data standards for coalition operations, or critical software dependencies that affect multiple allied AI systems.

○ **Sun Tzu's Counsel (Adapted):** Form alliances; ensure AI systems are interoperable and data can be shared securely and efficiently. A failure in AI interoperability on this ground can lead to fratricide by algorithm or an inability to mount a cohesive defence or offence.

1. **Serious Ground** (*Zhong Di*): *When AI forces have penetrated deeply into adversary systems, with many fortified enemy AI defences behind them.*

○ **AI Context:** A successful cyber operation has gained access to core enemy command and control networks, or autonomous systems operate deep within contested physical territory, relying on tenuous data links.

○ **Sun Tzu's Counsel (Adapted):** Ensure a continuous flow of "digital plunder"—that is, secure the necessary data, processing power, and bandwidth to sustain the AI's operation and exfiltrate intelligence. Focus on AI self-preservation and achieving the primary objective before withdrawal.

1. **Difficult ground** (*Pi Di*): *Digital environments that are inherently hard to operate AI in, such as heavily jammed electromagnetic spectrums, networks with extreme latency, or areas where data is scarce or unreliable.*

○ **AI Context:** Operations in dense urban canyons disrupting GPS and communications for drones, or cyber operations against air-gapped networks.

○ **Sun Tzu's Counsel (Adapted):** Keep steadily on the march. Employ AI systems designed for resilience and autonomous operation in degraded conditions. Progress may be slow, but maintaining AI functionality and adapting to the problematic "terrain" is key.

1. **Hemmed-in Ground** (*Wei Di*): *Where AI assets are trapped, with limited avenues for extraction or reinforcement, and vulnerable to adversary AI countermeasures.*

○ **AI Context:** An AI-controlled drone swarm is caught in an electronic warfare ambush, or a cyber exploitation tool is detected and isolated within an enemy network.

○ **Sun Tzu's Counsel (Adapted):** Resort to stratagem. Use AI to create diversions, feign new capabilities, or find unconventional escape routes. This might involve AI autonomously altering its behaviour to confuse pursuers or sacrificing some assets to allow others to withdraw.

1. **Desperate ground** (*Si Di*): *When AI systems face imminent destruction or compromise, and inaction guarantees catastrophic failure.*

○ **AI Context:** A critical command AI is about to be overwhelmed by a cyberattack, or autonomous defensive systems are the last line of defence against an incoming barrage.

○ **Sun Tzu's Counsel (Adapted):** Fight. Unleash the full capabilities of the AI, even if it involves high-risk automated actions or the expenditure of all remaining resources. On desperate ground, the AI's programming should prioritise mission success or critical asset survival above all else, within its ethical and legal constraints.

Understanding these nine situations in their AI context allows the commander to anticipate challenges, prepare appropriate responses, and guide the application of intelligent systems with greater foresight and adaptability, turning potential peril into strategic opportunity.

XII. Attack by Fire (and Code): AI in Destructive and Disruptive Operations (Huo Gong)

Sun Tzu dedicated a chapter to attack by fire, recognising its devastating psychological and physical impact. In the modern era, "fire" retains its literal meaning, now often guided with AI-enhanced precision, but it also finds resonant analogues in the destructive and disruptive capabilities of AI in the cyber and electronic domains. The principles of using such potent tools—timing, preparation, and exploiting the enemy's disorder—remain strikingly relevant.

AI-Guided Kinetic "Fire":

- **Precision Targeting:** AI algorithms can analyse sensor data (electro-optical, infrared, radar, signals intelligence) to identify, classify, and track targets with remarkable speed and accuracy. This enables more precise application of kinetic force, potentially reducing collateral damage if ethical considerations and accurate data are paramount. AI can assist in selecting the optimal weapon and impact point to achieve the desired effect.

- **Autonomous Engagement:** Lethal Autonomous Weapons (LAWs) represent the capacity for AI to independently select and engage targets once activated by a human. Systems like Close-In Weapon System (CIWS) on naval vessels or active protection systems on tanks already employ such autonomy for defensive purposes. Extending offensive autonomous capabilities is a significant and ethically fraught development.

- **Swarm Attacks:** AI can coordinate swarms of armed drones to deliver synchronised kinetic attacks, overwhelming defences through sheer numbers and multi-axis approaches.

Attack by "Code" – Cyber and Electronic "Fire":

The digital equivalent of an attack by fire aims to cripple, disrupt, or destroy an adversary's information infrastructure, command and control systems, and AI-dependent capabilities.

- **Destructive Cyber Attacks:** AI can develop and deploy highly sophisticated malware designed to erase data, corrupt firmware, or cause physical damage to industrial control systems (a "digital Stuxnet"). The speed and adaptability of AI can make these attacks harder to defend against.

- **Denial of Service/Access:** Overwhelming enemy servers, communication nodes, or AI processing units with floods of data, effectively "burning out" their capacity or denying access to critical resources.

- **Electronic Warfare as "Fire":** High-powered microwave weapons or advanced jamming techniques, potentially guided by AI to identify and target critical enemy frequencies, can disable or permanently damage sensitive electronic components in enemy AI systems, sensors, and communication devices. This is akin to starting a fire in the enemy's electronic arsenal.

- **Data Incineration/Corruption:** Targeting and destroying or irrecoverably corrupting an adversary's critical datasets (e.g., AI training data, intelligence databases, command archives) can have a devastating and lasting impact on their ability to wage AI-driven warfare.

Principles for Attack by Fire and Code:

Sun Tzu's conditions for fire attacks find echoes in the digital domain:

- **"When the people are unsettled":** Launch cyber-attacks when the enemy's networks are known to be unstable, undergoing maintenance, or when their cyber defenders are distracted or overwhelmed.

- **"When provisions are gathered":** Target data centres or communication hubs when critical data is being aggregated or transmitted.

- **"When the army is encamped":** Attack enemy systems in a static, configured state, rather than when they are dynamically reconfiguring or on high alert.

- **Exploit the Disorder:** The chaos caused by a successful fire or code attack should be exploited immediately with follow-on actions, whether kinetic or non-kinetic. AI can help identify the optimal moment and means for this exploitation.

Using such powerful, destructive and disruptive tools, whether kinetic fire guided by AI or digital "fire" delivered by code, demands extreme caution. The potential for rapid escalation, unintended consequences (e.g., cyberattacks spreading beyond their intended targets), and severe violations of IHL (particularly regarding distinction and proportionality) is immense. The wise commander employs these methods only when the objective is critical, the conditions are favourable, and the potential repercussions have been thoroughly weighed. This ensures that such attacks serve a clear strategic purpose and remain under ultimate human control and responsibility.

XIII. The Use of Spies (AI-Powered Intelligence) (Yong Jian)

"Spy operations are essential in war; upon them the army relies to make its every move," declared Sun Tzu, underscoring the supreme importance of intelligence. In the age of AI, the role of the "spy" is transformed and amplified, with intelligent systems becoming the primary gatherers, processors, and even predictors of enemy actions and intentions. Protecting one's digital secrets and understanding the adversary's AI-driven intelligence capabilities are the new frontiers of espionage and counter-espionage.

AI as the Omnipresent Spy:

- **Intelligence, Surveillance, and Reconnaissance (ISR) Revolutionised:** AI algorithms sift through colossal volumes of data from a myriad of sensors—satellite imagery, drone footage, signals intercepts, ground sensors, and Open Source Intelligence (OSINT). AI can detect patterns, identify objects (e.g., specific military hardware), track movements, and flag anomalies at speeds and scales far beyond human capacity. This provides unprecedented situational awareness.

- **Predictive Analytics as Foresight:** Machine learning models, trained on historical data and current intelligence, can forecast potential enemy courses of action, identify likely ambush sites, or predict logistical bottlenecks. This AI-driven foresight allows commanders to anticipate and pre-empt enemy moves, a modern realisation of Sun Tzu's ideal of knowing the enemy's plans.

- **Cyber Espionage:** AI-powered tools can automate aspects of network infiltration, data exfiltration, and the monitoring of adversary communications. They can identify vulnerabilities for exploitation and sift through captured data to find critical intelligence.

- **Natural Language Processing (NLP) and Computer Vision:** These AI disciplines are crucial for intelligence extraction. NLP can analyse text from intercepted communications or social media in multiple languages, while computer vision processes images and videos from drones and satellites. The Ukrainian acoustic reconnaissance system Zvook and text analysis tool Griselda exemplify such applications.

The New Counterintelligence:

With AI playing such a central role in intelligence, counterintelligence efforts must adapt:

- **Protecting Algorithms and Training Data:** One's own AI algorithms and the datasets used to train them become highly valuable secrets. Adversaries will seek to steal, reverse-engineer, or corrupt these assets. Robust cybersecurity and data governance are essential counterintelligence measures.

- **Detecting AI-Driven Surveillance:** Developing capabilities to detect and counter adversary AI-ISR systems, including camouflaging assets against AI recognition or spoofing AI sensors.

- **Algorithmic Verification and Data Integrity:** Ensuring that one's AI systems are not being fed manipulated data or that their algorithms have not been subtly compromised is a critical new counterintelligence task. The "double agent" of the AI era could be a compromised AI system unknowingly feeding false intelligence to its own side. This necessitates continuous validation of AI outputs and security audits of AI systems.

The shift from primarily human intelligence gathering to machine-speed collection and analysis presents immense opportunities and significant challenges. While AI can provide a deluge of information, the human analyst's role evolves to focus on critical interpretation, validating AI-generated insights, understanding context that machines might miss, and managing the risk of information overload or over-reliance on potentially flawed AI. The commander must cultivate an intelligence apparatus where human expertise and machine capability work in synergy, ensuring that the "spies" of the st century provide clear, actionable, and trustworthy intelligence. The highest form of intelligence in this new age is not just knowing what the enemy possesses, but understanding the logic, biases, and vulnerabilities of the AI systems they rely on.

Table : Sun Tzu's Principles Reimagined for AI Warfare

Sun Tzu's Principle	AI-Era Interpretation
Moral Law/ Alignment (◈)	Ethical AI programming, IHL/ROE compliance, public/ allied trust in AI systems, alignment with political objectives.
Heaven (◈)	Digital environment dynamics: network latency, bandwidth, processing cycles, cyber threat "weather," technological obsolescence cycles.
Earth (◈)	Cyber-physical landscape: network architectures, data centres, cloud infrastructure, spectrum, data topographies, server locations.
Commander (◈)	Human-AI leadership: understanding AI capabilities/limits, fostering trust in human-AI teams, managing cognitive load, ensuring meaningful human control.
Method/ Discipline (◈)	AI Ecosystem: doctrines, TTPs, software development cycles, data governance, cybersecurity protocols, AI training, logistical support for AI.
Deception (◈◈)	AI-driven cyber/information operations, deepfakes, feigning computational weakness/strength, masking intrusions, generating misleading patterns.
Use of Spies (◈◈)	AI-powered ISR, predictive analytics, cyber espionage, OSINT analysis, understanding adversary AI capabilities/ limitations.
Terrain (◈ ◈)	Digital (network/data/spectrum/software topology) and Cognitive (information environment, belief systems, human-machine interface) landscapes.
Speed (◈)	Computational speed, algorithmic efficiency, rapid adaptation, accelerated OODA loops, and swift deployment of digital effects.

Sun Tzu's Principle	AI-Era Interpretation
Weakness/ Strength (� �)	Algorithmic bias, software vulnerabilities, data dependencies (weakness); resilient networks, unbiased AI, diverse data, robust human oversight (strength).
Winning Without Fighting (�)	Non-kinetic effects (cyber, EW, info ops), degrading adversary trust in their AI, cognitive paralysis, and attacking enemy AI systems directly.
Force/Shi (�)	Algorithmic momentum from data dominance, superior algorithms, computational speed, integrated human-AI orchestration, and surprise via AI novelty.
Manoeuvring (��)	AI-enabled autonomous navigation (physical), network infiltration/lateral movement (cyber), targeted information operations (cognitive).
Attack by fire (��)	AI-guided precision kinetic strikes, destructive cyber attacks (data/firmware destruction), and advanced electronic warfare.

Conclusion: Enduring Wisdom in the Face of Intelligent Machines

Artificial Intelligence's advent has altered warfare's character, introducing capabilities and complexities at a scale and speed previously confined to the realm of speculation. Algorithms now sift through intelligence, guide autonomous systems, orchestrate defences, and wage battles in the unseen domain of cyberspace. Yet, as this treatise has sought to demonstrate, the fundamental *nature* of war—as a violent expression of political will, a clash of human intellects and passions, fraught with uncertainty and friction—endures. The timeless principles articulated by Sun Tzu, born from an age of chariots and bronze, retain their profound relevance in this new epoch of sentient code.

The core teachings—the imperative of thorough planning and assessment based on fundamental factors; the supreme importance of knowing oneself and the enemy;the value of deception and surprise; the wisdom of attacking the enemy's strategy and subduing them without prolonged fighting, the necessity of speed, adaptability, and exploiting weakness, and the critical role of intelligence —all find new and potent applications in AI-driven conflict. The "Moral Alignment" demands ethically sound AI, "Digital Heaven" and "Networked Earth" redefine the operational environment; the "Human-AI Commander" faces new leadership challenges; and the "AI Ecosystem" becomes the bedrock of "Method and Protocols" .

However, integrating AI is neither a panacea nor a purely technical endeavour. It introduces novel challenges: the risk of information overload overwhelming human cognition, the danger of algorithmic bias leading to flawed or unjust outcomes, the potential for rapid, unintended escalation due to machine-speed interactions, the complexities of maintaining meaningful human control over lethal autonomous systems, and the ever-present threat of adversarial manipulation of one's own AI. These challenges underscore that human wisdom, ethical judgment, political purpose, and understanding the enduring human element, including its cognitive limitations and psychological dimensions, remain paramount.

To view AI merely as a superior tool is to miss its more profound strategic implications. The true art lies not in building the most powerful or fastest algorithm, but in cultivating the wisdom to wield these potent capabilities responsibly and effectively, in harmony with overarching strategic goals and ethical principles. This requires a new generation of leaders who are adept in both the art of strategy and the science of intelligent systems and capable of discerning the opportunities AI presents while guarding against its inherent perils.

As human-AI teaming evolves and autonomous systems become more prevalent, the lines between human and machine strategy may blur, potentially leading to unforeseen emergent behaviours and new forms of conflict. To navigate this future, where the character of war will continue to evolve and perhaps even challenge aspects of its perceived nature, requires proactive engagement today. By embedding enduring principles of strategy, ethics, and control into the very fabric of AI development and military doctrine, we can strive to ensure that these intelligent machines remain our servants, not our masters, in the complex and perilous arena of war. The ultimate victory, as always, will belong not to those who possess the most advanced technology, but to those who wield it with the most extraordinary wisdom, foresight, and understanding of the unchanging Tao of conflict.

Exclusive Bonus Print Book Chapter - Sun Tzu's Art of Social Media: Ancient Wisdom in the Digital Age

If Sun Tzu, the ancient Chinese general and philosopher, were to pen *The Art of War* in the 21st century, his strategic gaze would undoubtedly fall upon the vast and influential battleground of social media. Far from a mere distraction, he would recognize it as a critical domain for intelligence, influence, and achieving victory, often without direct confrontation.

1. All Warfare is Based on Deception (Social Media Edition): Sun Tzu would master the art of perception management. This would involve:

- **Crafting Narratives:** Creating and disseminating narratives that shape public opinion and portray oneself or one's cause in the most favourable light, while subtly undermining opponents.
- **Illusory Engagement:** Using bots, sock puppet accounts (with caution, as discovery could backfire), or coordinated inauthentic behaviour to create an illusion of widespread support or opposition.
- **Strategic Silence and Misdirection:** Knowing when *not* to post, or posting content designed to mislead opponents about one's true intentions, focus, or capabilities. Appearing weak when strong in certain online discussions, or strong when actually vulnerable,

to lure adversaries into miscalculation.

- **Meme Warfare and Virality:** Leveraging humour, relatable content, and emotionally resonant messages to spread ideas rapidly and organically, making them appear as grassroots movements rather than orchestrated campaigns.

2. Know Your Enemy and Know Yourself (The Digital Dossier): Sun Tzu's famous dictum would extend to the meticulous analysis of the social media landscape:

- **Social Listening and Sentiment Analysis:** Employing sophisticated tools to monitor conversations, identify key influencers, understand public sentiment towards various topics, and gauge the emotional responses to events or messages. This is the new "ground" and "weather."
- **Opponent Profiling:** Analysing the social media presence of adversaries – their messaging, supporter base, engagement patterns, vulnerabilities, and even the personal habits or psychological triggers of key figures.
- **Self-Assessment:** Understanding one's own online strengths, weaknesses, follower demographics, and the potential reach and impact of one's own social media channels. Recognizing one's own "echo chambers" and information bubbles.

3. Subdue the Enemy Without Fighting (Winning Hearts and Minds Online): The ultimate victory for Sun Tzu was one achieved without bloodshed. On social media, this translates to:

- **Psychological Operations (PsyOps):** Disseminating information (or disinformation, if aligned with his principles of deception for a greater strategic goal) to sway the opinions, emotions, and ultimately, the actions of a target audience. This could involve highlighting an opponent's contradictions, fuelling internal dissent within their ranks, or fostering a sense of hopelessness among their supporters.
- **Building Alliances and Networks:** Identifying and cultivating relationships with influential accounts, online communities, and micro-influencers who can amplify messages and lend credibility.
- **Shaping the Narrative Pre-emptively:** Establishing a strong, positive online presence and defining the terms of discussion before a crisis or conflict arises, making it harder for opponents to land their attacks.
- **Targeted Messaging:** Tailoring content to specific audience segments to maximize resonance and persuasive power, rather than using a one-size-fits-all approach.

4. The Supreme Importance of Intelligence (Spies in the Digital Realm): Information is power, and Sun Tzu would exploit social media as a vast intelligence-gathering network:

- **Open-Source Intelligence (OSINT):** Mining

publicly available information from social media profiles, posts, and connections to gather intelligence on individuals, organizations, or even troop movements (as seen in modern conflicts).

- **Identifying Key Nodes and Influencers:** Recognizing that not all voices are equal, he would focus on identifying and understanding (or influencing) the key individuals and groups who shape opinion and information flow within relevant networks.
- **Early Warning Systems:** Monitoring social media for emerging threats, burgeoning crises, or shifts in public opinion that could signal future challenges or opportunities.

5. Avoid Prolonged Conflict (The Perils of Endless Online Battles): Sun Tzu warned against wars of attrition. On social media, this means:

- **Strategic Engagement and Disengagement:** Choosing battles wisely. Not every criticism or provocation warrants a response. Knowing when to engage, when to ignore, and when to strategically withdraw or de-escalate to conserve resources and avoid unproductive flame wars.
- **Swift and Decisive Action (When Necessary):** If a direct online confrontation is unavoidable, the aim should be to achieve objectives quickly and decisively, then control the subsequent narrative.
- **Preventing Burnout:** Recognizing that sustained

online campaigns can be exhausting for those involved and can lead to diminishing returns.

6. Speed and Adaptability (The 24/7 News Cycle): The digital landscape changes rapidly. Sun Tzu would emphasize:

- **Rapid Response Capabilities:** Having the ability to react quickly to developing events, misinformation, or attacks on one's reputation.
- **Flexibility in Tactics:** Being prepared to change messaging, platforms, or approaches as the online environment and audience behaviour evolve. What works today might be ineffective tomorrow.
- **Exploiting "Unguarded Moments":** Capitalizing on an opponent's social media gaffes, poorly received statements, or moments of weakness.

7. Use of Direct and Indirect Methods (Content Mix): Not all communication should be confrontational:

- **Direct Engagement:** Openly stating positions, refuting claims, and engaging in public debate when advantageous.
- **Indirect Influence:** Sharing third-party endorsements, positive news stories, or subtly shaping conversations through curated content and strategic placement of information. Creating "soft power" through cultural or human-interest content.

8. Discipline and Cohesion (Managing the Message): Even in a decentralized environment, Sun Tzu would stress:

- **Message Discipline:** Ensuring that all official or affiliated accounts are aligned in their core messaging, even if the tone is adapted for different platforms or audiences.
- **Training and Preparation:** Educating those who manage social media on strategic objectives, potential pitfalls, and best practices for online conduct and engagement.

In essence, Sun Tzu would view social media as a powerful tool for shaping the "moral law" (the will of the people and their alignment with leadership), for understanding the "terrain" (the digital landscape and its communities), and for employing "stratagems" to achieve strategic objectives with maximum efficiency and minimal direct confrontation. His *Art of War* for the social media age would be a masterclass in influence, intelligence, and the subtle art of winning before the battle is overtly joined.

www.ingramcontent.com/pod-product-compliance
Lightning Source LLC
LaVergne TN
LVHW090429210926
848480LV00002B/743

* 9 7 9 8 2 3 1 2 8 8 8 6 1 *